CONTENTS

Words that appear in the text in bold, **like this**, are explained in the glossary.

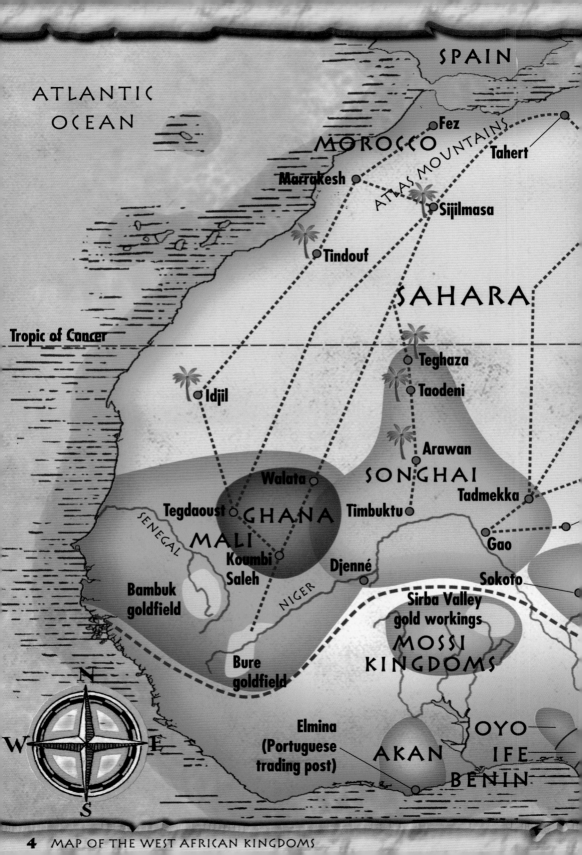

SPAIN

ATLANTIC
OCEAN

MOROCCO

Fez

Tahert

Marrakesh

ATLAS MOUNTAINS

Sijilmasa

Tindouf

SAHARA

Tropic of Cancer

Teghaza

Idjil

Taodeni

Arawan

SONGHAI

Walata

Tadmekka

SENEGAL

Tegdaoust

GHANA

Timbuktu

MALI

Gao

Koumbi
Saleh

Djenné

Sokoto

NIGER

Bambuk
goldfield

Sirba Valley
gold workings

Bure
goldfield

MOSSI
KINGDOMS

N

W   E

Elmina
(Portuguese
trading post)

AKAN

OYO
IFE
BENIN

S

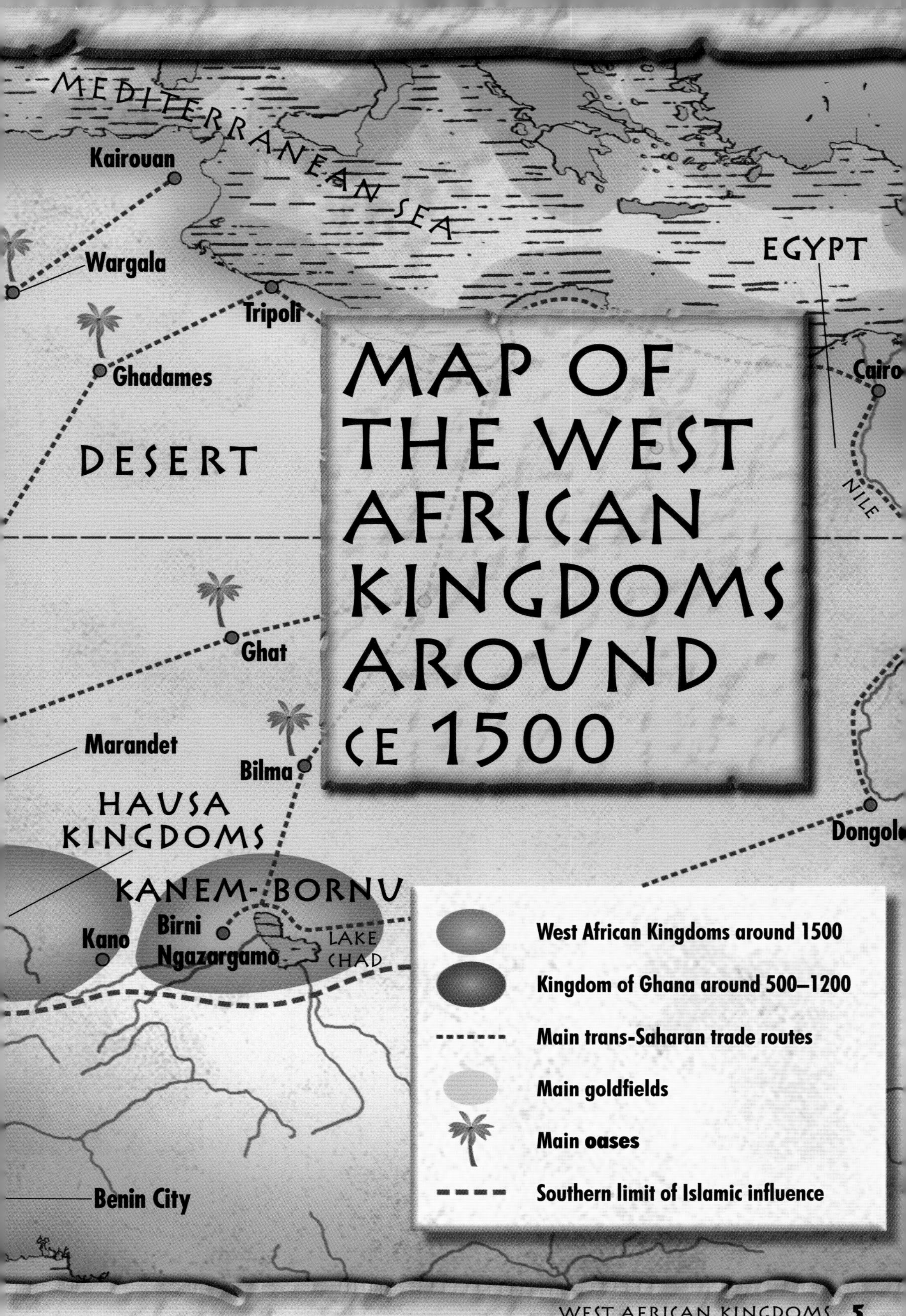

MAP OF THE WEST AFRICAN KINGDOMS CE 1500

Kairouan

Wargala

Tripoli

Ghadames

DESERT

EGYPT

Cairo

NILE

Ghat

Marandet

Bilma

HAUSA KINGDOMS

KANEM-BORNU

Kano

Birni Ngazargamo

LAKE CHAD

Dongola

Benin City

MEDITERRANEAN SEA

	West African Kingdoms around 1500
	Kingdom of Ghana around 500–1200
-------	Main trans-Saharan trade routes
	Main goldfields
🌴	Main oases
- - - -	Southern limit of Islamic influence

The Great Mosque at Djenné was first built in the 13th century. That was more than 700 years ago.

CHAPTER 1

FACTS ABOUT WEST AFRICA

Europeans used to call Africa the "Dark Continent." They thought it was dangerous and wild. Come and visit West Africa's kingdoms (states) of gold and find out how wrong they were. Enjoy great festivals, music, and dance. You will also discover all sorts of exciting wildlife.

Learn some of the language and make friends. Traveling around is generally safe, but do look after your health. Tropical diseases can ruin even the best vacations.

WHEN TO TRAVEL

The West African Kingdoms were great kingdoms for more than 1,000 years. The best time to visit is between CE 1200 and 1600. That is between 400 and 800 years ago.

ORIGINS OF THE WEST AFRICAN KINGDOMS

Travel between CE 500 and 1200 to see the beginnings of West African **civilization**, or society. That is between 800 and 1,500 years ago. The first kingdoms, such as Ghana, developed on the edge of the Sahara Desert (see map, pages 4–5).

Arab traders from North Africa began to visit this region to buy gold, **ivory**, and slaves. Slaves have no freedom. Arab traders also introduced the West Africans to their Arabic writing and Islamic religion. Followers of **Islam** worship one God, called Allah.

THE GOLDEN AGE

Visit the region between CE 1200 and 1600. That is between 400 and 800 years ago. You will see the West African Kingdoms at their very best. Mali and Songhai are the most powerful kingdoms (see map, pages 4–5). They trade goods, such as gold and copper, with North Africa. Smaller kingdoms, such as Benin and Oyo, begin to develop during this time. They are in the forests near the coast.

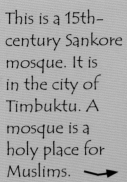

This is a 15th-century Sankore mosque. It is in the city of Timbuktu. A mosque is a holy place for Muslims. →

DECLINE OF THE WEST AFRICAN KINGDOMS

400 years ago the West African Kingdoms begin to **decline** (fade). Other countries start to conquer the area. Raids and kidnappings by slave traders are a danger. So are holy wars, or battles over religious differences. This decline happened from 1600 to 1900.

GOOD AND BAD TIMES TO VISIT

500–1200	First kingdoms develop on the edge of the Sahara Desert.
1200–1600	West African Kingdoms are at their height.
1713–1807	Atlantic Ocean slave trade is at its height.
1804–1864	**Muslim** kingdoms fight **jihads** (holy wars) against their non-Muslim neighbours (who do not follow Islam).
1880–1900	Europeans conquer West Africa.

Key:

Stay away   Interesting times to visit   Best times to visit

This is a view over the savanna from the rocky Bandiagara cliff in Mali.

CLIMATE AND LANDSCAPE

West Africa has two main types of landscape. They have two different climates. The north (see map, pages 4–5) has a type of tropical grassland and woods, called **savanna**. The northern edge merges with desert. Between the savanna and the Atlantic Ocean is a **rain forest** zone. The rain forest is an area of dense tropical forest with plenty of rain.

SEASONS

The West African year is divided into wet and dry seasons. The dry season is from November to March. The wet season is from April to October. Avoid traveling in the wet season. The **humidity** (moist, damp air) will make you feel very uncomfortable. Also the rains turn the roads into mud.

The people living in the rain forest and the savanna have developed different ways of life.

HERDING ON THE SAVANNA

During the Golden Age (see page 8), the savanna is ideal for farming. The grain **millet** is grown in drier areas. Rice is grown near the rivers. The savanna provides good grazing for herds of cattle, sheep, and goats. There are plenty of wild animals to hunt.

NATURAL RESOURCES
The West African Kingdoms are rich in gold. West Africa also has many other valuable resources including copper, iron, **ivory**, and salt.

FARMING IN THE FORESTS

Farmers cut down trees in the tropical forests. This creates fields for crops. Crops grow fast in the hot, wet climate. The forest soils lose their fertility, or richness, after a few years of farming though. Then the farmers clear new fields. The forest grows back over the old fields, and the soil begins to get rich once again. Important crops include bananas, **plantains** (like big bananas), and rice.

Plantains are popular throughout the West African Kingdoms.

ANCIENT KINGDOMS

In the Golden Age period (see page 8), West Africa is divided into many smaller kingdoms. Watch to see how the culture (way of life) is different in these varied kingdoms.

GHANA

Visit Ghana to see the first large kingdom in West Africa. Ghana was founded 1,500 years ago, in about CE 500. Ideally visit between 750 and 1100. That is around 1000 years ago. The **Islam** religion begins to become more powerful. The modern country of Ghana is not related to the old kingdom of Ghana.

MALI

Mali was the first great **Muslim** kingdom of West Africa. Mali was founded about 1,000 years ago, in CE 1000. 300 years later, Mansa Musa is Mali's ruler (see box, below). Mali controls all of West Africa's most important trading cities. These trading cities include Timbuktu and Gao.

GIFTS OF GOLD

Over 600 years ago (in the 14th century), Mali is an extremely wealthy region. Mansa Musa's reign is a very good time to visit. He is a generous ruler, and foreign visitors to his court often receive presents of gold.

SONGHAI

The capital of Songhai is Gao. Over 500 years ago, King Sonni Ali led **cavalry** raids (on horseback) against his neighbors. He turned the kingdom of Songhai into a major power. Songhai became rich because of its control of trade (buying and selling) in the Sahara Desert (see map, pages 4–5). Songhai was invaded and taken over by the country of Morocco in 1591. That was over 400 years ago.

BENIN

Benin was once one of the most powerful kingdoms of the Nigerian **rain forest**. It was at its peak about 550 years ago. Benin survived until just over 100 years ago, in 1897. This is when it was conquered by Britain. In Benin you will see some of the most brilliant art and craft works in West Africa.

This bronze **plaque** from Benin shows a king (center) with his servants.

ISLAM

Islam is the main religion in the northern kingdoms. It was founded about 1,400 years ago by the Arab **prophet** Muhammad. A prophet believes he speaks for his God. Followers of Islam are called **Muslims**. They worship one God, known as Allah. North African traders introduced Islam to the region in about CE 1000. That was around 1,000 years ago. West Africans have gradually changed the religion to suit their own lifestyle.

VISIT AN AMAZING MUD MOSQUE

minaret

Muslims use buildings called mosques for special prayers on Fridays. This is the holy day. In West Africa many mosques have been made from mud. Sticks poke out of the walls. Workers can climb up on the sticks to repair the building. Mosques have a prayer hall and a **minaret** (tower).

The minaret of the Great Mosque at Djenné. The mosque is made of mud.

RAMADAN

In Muslim areas you need to be aware of the month of Ramadan. During Ramadan, Muslims **fast**. They must not eat or drink between sunrise and sunset. They may not like it if you eat, either. Ramadan occurs at a different time every year, so check before you go.

ISLAMIC LEARNING

Islamic kingdoms are the only ones in West Africa to use writing before CE 1600. That is about 400 years ago. Muslim students learn how to write using the Arabic alphabet. Students also learn the Arabic language. They can then study the Qur'an and the teachings of Muhammad. The Qur'an is the holy book of Islam.

This 15th-century Islamic text is from the city of Timbuktu. The text is over 500 years old.

TRADITIONAL RELIGIONS

There are many different beliefs in West African traditional religions. Most of these beliefs include a single, supreme (all-powerful) god. Human prayers cannot even reach this god. Locals prefer to worship the hundreds of lesser gods and spirits. They believe that these gods and spirits can influence the supreme god to help them.

YORUBA GODS

Every African **ethnic group** has its own gods. An ethnic group is a group with the same culture. The Yoruba people are a major Nigerian ethnic group. Here are just a few of their 401 gods.

Olorun: the supreme god. Olorun fixes everyone's destiny (fortune). He also decides how long a person will live. Those who live good lives are reborn in a new body. Those who live bad lives go to a place of punishment.

Obatala: the second-highest god after Olorun. He molded the first men and women out of clay.

Oya: goddess of the Niger River and of wind.

Olokun: the god of the sea.

Ogun: the fierce god of iron and war. He protects blacksmiths, hunters, and warriors.

Shango: god of thunder and lightning.

Eshu: messenger god. He is a trickster, so he must not be insulted.

Yemoja: goddess of rivers, streams, and lakes.

Oshun: a goddess who protects women during childbirth.

Offerings are made to the spirits at this shrine in the kingdom of Mali.

THE LIVING DEAD

Just because someone is dead does not mean they are gone forever. West Africans believe the spirits of the dead live on in their old homes. West Africans have deep respect for these spirits.

Wood and stone carvings of **ancestor** figures are kept in shrines, or temples. Ancestors are relatives from the past. People can go to ask the spirits for advice or help. West Africans may sacrifice (kill) animals to keep the spirits happy.

RULERS AND SOCIETY

West African rulers get their power from the supreme god. Kings also often act as priests. Sometimes they are thought to have magical powers.

THE RANKS OF SOCIETY

In most West African Kingdoms, people hold different ranks or positions. The king and his family have the highest rank. Below the king are local chiefs. Chiefs perform services and pay taxes. These taxes are fees paid to the king. Below the chiefs are ordinary men and women. These include merchants (traders) and farmers. They all pay taxes to the chiefs. Slaves have the lowest rank (see pages 20–21).

MANNERS AT COURT

Visitors to the king must show great respect. You should go down on your knees, or even on all fours. Do not talk directly to the king. Speak to an attendant. The attendant will pass on the king's words to you.

WOMEN IN WEST AFRICA

In the West African Kingdoms, family names are thought to be inherited (passed down) from the mother's family. Rank is also thought to be inherited from the mother's family. Rank is important in Africa. Women still have to work hard every day though. They plant and harvest crops. They fetch water, cook, and bring up the children.

WAR

Wars between the West African Kingdoms are quite common. The **cavalry** (soldiers on horseback) is the most important part of any army in the **savanna**. The cavalrymen fight with lances and swords. In the **rain forest** regions, soldiers fight on foot. They fight with bows and poisoned arrows and spears.

People carry a modern West African king in a parade. They are celebrating a **yam** festival (see page 41). The red umbrellas are symbols, or signs, of royal power.

SLAVERY

Slavery is a fact of life throughout the West African Kingdoms. As a visitor to the region, this will be the hardest custom (practice) for you to accept.

WHO CAN BECOME A SLAVE?

Slaves work for other people. They are not paid and have no freedom. A person can become a slave as a punishment for a crime. Powerful West African rulers may attack their neighbors to capture people. These people can then be sold as slaves. A slave's children will become slaves, too.

SLAVES' RIGHTS

Slaves are the property of their owner. But they do have certain human rights. A slave must be fed, clothed, and treated properly. If not, he can be set free.

These iron rings fasten around slaves' ankles. The rings are to stop slaves from escaping.

IMPROVING SLAVES' LIVES

An owner can allow his slave to marry. Slave families usually stay together. Slaves can own property, including other slaves, and run their own business. A successful slave can even buy his freedom. **Muslims** believe that freeing slaves is a way to please God.

This is the slave house on Gorée Island in the country of Senegal. It was built by the Dutch in 1776. Slaves were kept here before they were shipped to the Caribbean.

WHAT TO WEAR

In the Islamic north, men and women cover up. They prefer not to show their skin. Clothes also protect them from the hot sun. In the south, people wear fewer clothes. You can even walk naked in some places. Colorful fabrics and fancy jewelry are popular everywhere. People in the trading cities are used to visitors. But take care in more remote areas.

If you are white, West Africans may not have seen your skin color before. At this time, they may think you are a spirit and react with fear.

turban

MUSLIM AREAS

Men wear loose white cotton shirts and baggy pants. They cover their shirts with a long, loose red garment. It is called a **caftan**. Over that they usually wear a short, striped vest. They wear red leather shoes and on their head a white turban.

This Tuareg man from Timbuktu wears loose clothes. They are very similar to those worn hundreds of years ago in West Africa.

WOMEN'S CLOTHES

Like the men, women wear a long, cotton caftan over their clothes. Underneath they wear another long, cotton garment. They always wear a head scarf but not a veil. They also wear red leather shoes. Both men and women wear gold earrings. Women wear gold bracelets around their arms and ankles.

RAIN FOREST AREAS

Do not pack many clothes for the **rain forest** kingdoms. Men and women go barefoot and prefer to wear a cotton skirt with a belt. Robes can be worn on special occasions. People dress simply, but wear jewelry. They like to wear bracelets and necklaces. These are made from gold, glass, shells, and brass. Women braid, bead, or shave their hair. Men are usually clean-shaven.

Women in Mali today still wear gold and amber hair decorations.

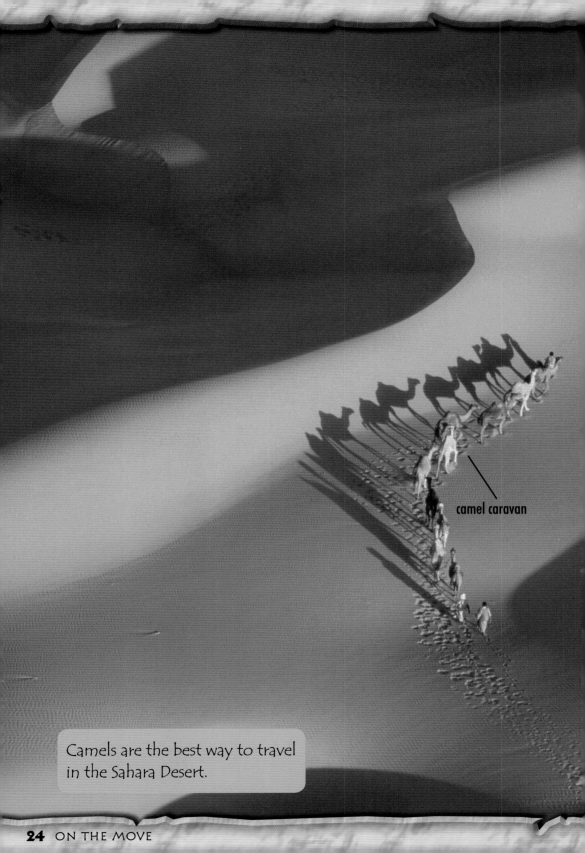

camel caravan

Camels are the best way to travel in the Sahara Desert.

CHAPTER 2

ON THE MOVE

Travel across the Sahara Desert by **camel caravan** to the West African Kingdoms. The journey's hot and tiring, but well worth it. You'll find friendly faces at the caravan cities as you travel. There will be a good choice of clean and comfortable places to stay. Food is simple, but filling. Visit after 1600 and enjoy the new crops such as corn (maize). That is about 400 years ago.

HOW TO GET THERE

Getting to the West African Kingdoms is the most difficult part. Before the late 1400s, the only option is to go from North Africa. That was over 500 years ago. This means a very tiring trek across the Sahara Desert with a **camel caravan**.

If you're traveling any later than the 1400s, you may be able to pick up a sailing ship from a European country. These ships can be cramped and dirty though. You may even end up arriving with a nasty disease called **scurvy**. This is caused by the lack of vitamin C in your diet.

CATCH A CAMEL

Camels make desert travel much easier. For safety in numbers, traders travel in camel caravans. You will see lines of camels making the difficult journey across the desert in this way.

Desert tribes can make raids on smaller groups of travelers. Pay the caravan leader before your trip. He will guide you safely across the desert from **oasis** (watering hole) to oasis. He may also provide armed guards. Desert nights can be freezing, so make sure you pack some warm clothes. Allow up to two months to travel from the coast of the Mediterranean Sea to the city of Timbuktu (see map, pages 4–5).

A caravan of camels rests in the desert. The caravan is close to its journey's end at Timbuktu.

GETTING ABOUT

To go places, most people walk. In the **savanna**, more wealthy people ride camels, donkeys, or horses. A camel is cheaper, but less comfortable, than a horse. You're unlikely to find any pack animals in the tropical forest. Only rulers and wealthy people can afford them. Another way to get around is in a **litter**. A litter is a bed or seat with handles used to carry people. Hire some porters to transport you and your luggage in style.

WHERE TO STAY

You will finally arrive in one of the great trading cities of the West African Kingdoms. You might arrive in Timbuktu (see map, pages 4–5). There will be plenty of places for tired travelers to sleep. Messengers travel ahead of your caravan to arrange a bed for you at a *funduq*, or inn.

STAY IN A *FUNDUQ*

Funduqs are good places for both merchants and travelers to stay. There are many different *funduqs* in Timbuktu. You will find dozens of guest rooms, a wash house, and a toilet block. Guest rooms are usually quite large rooms with high ceilings. Heat always rises so the lower part of the room stays a bit cooler. A *funduq* will be basic. You can expect a bed, clean sheets, and good washing facilities. Slaves or servants will do your laundry and also cook your meals.

PRIVATE HOMES

In most of the West African Kingdoms, you will have to make arrangements to stay in private homes. In the **savanna** region, houses are square with flat roofs. They are built of mud bricks. In the **rain forest** areas, homes consist of four separate, rectangular huts. They are around a central courtyard.

FAMILY COMPOUNDS

In savanna areas a home is often a round hut within a compound. A compound is a walled-in area with many places to live. The largest hut is for the head of the family. Men have more than one wife, and each wife has her own hut. The guest hut is near the entrance.

This picture shows a typical family compound built by the Nupe people of Nigeria.

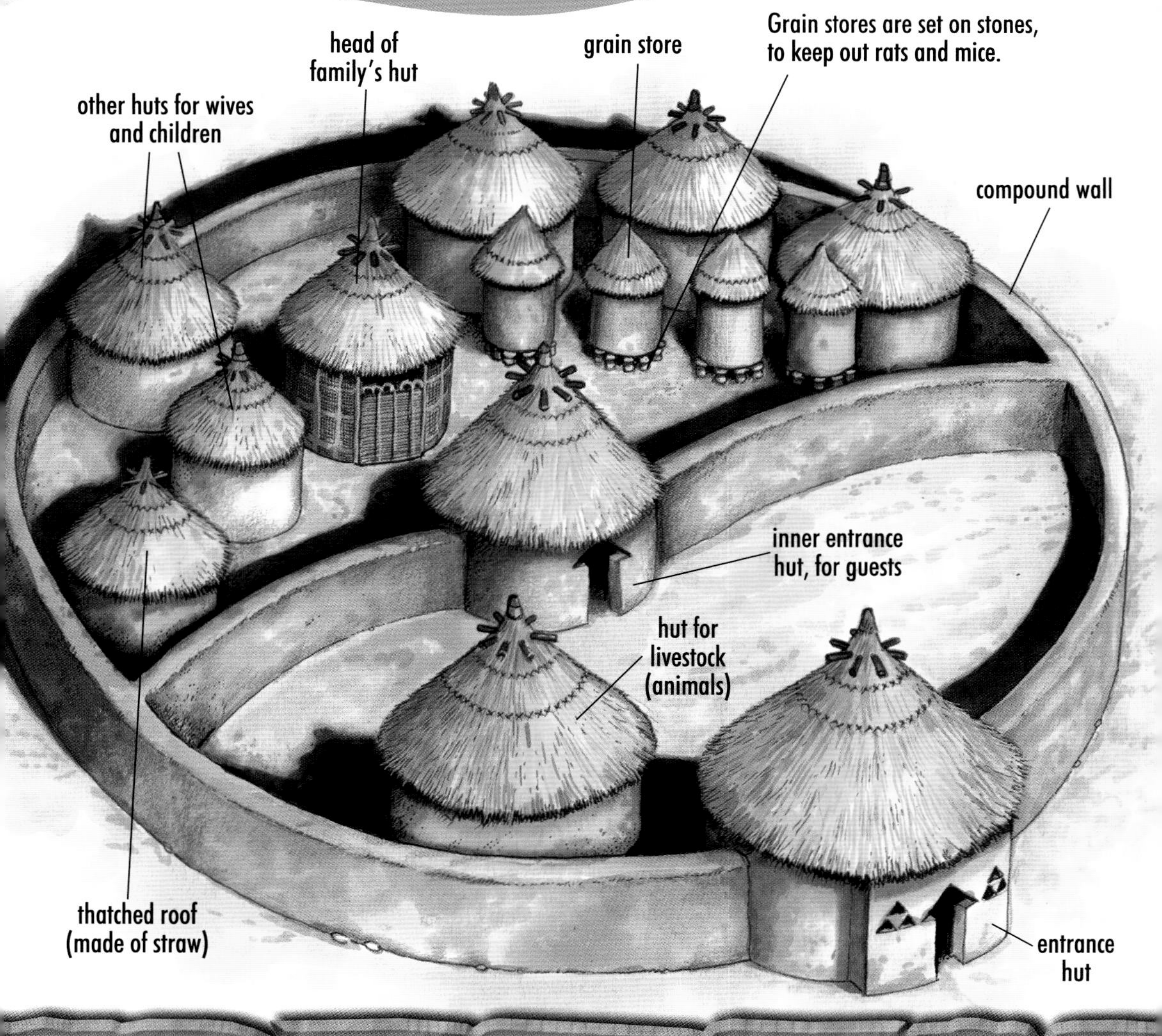

other huts for wives and children

head of family's hut

grain store

Grain stores are set on stones, to keep out rats and mice.

compound wall

inner entrance hut, for guests

hut for livestock (animals)

thatched roof (made of straw)

entrance hut

WHAT TO EAT

You will have a limited diet if you visit the West African Kingdoms before about 1600. That is about 400 years ago. In the **savanna** regions you will be offered rice, **millet** (grain), dairy products, and goat. In the **rain forest**, **yams**, **plantains**, bananas, and "bush meat" will be on the menu. Bush meat is from wild animals such as antelope, rats, and monkeys.

There's much more variety after 1600. New crops such as corn (maize), sweet potatoes, and chilies arrive from the Americas. In the south, be ready for spicy food, with lots of pepper. People eat three meals a day. They eat an early breakfast, main meal in mid-afternoon, and supper soon after sunset.

GOOD MANNERS

Your hosts in a **Muslim** city will offer you a welcoming meal. It will include millet mixed with honey and milk. Do not refuse this meal. Sharing food like this is a friendly gesture.

Don't feel insulted if your hosts touch your food with their mouth before giving it to you. This sign of good faith shows you the food is not poisoned. Always remember to wash your hands thoroughly before eating. In some places, men and women eat separately.

WHAT TO DRINK

Safe drinking water is hard to find in the West African Kingdoms. Most locals avoid water as it often gives them stomachaches. They prefer weak beer made from millet and honey. The beer-making process makes the water safer to drink. In Muslim areas you will be offered milk or water. The **Islam** religion forbids the drinking of alcohol. Stick to the milk.

A woman prepares the family meal on an outdoor stove. Most cooking is done outdoors in the West African Kingdoms.

These handmade baskets are woven from dried grass. Baskets like these have been made and sold in West African street markets for centuries.

CHAPTER 3

WHERE TO GO AND WHAT TO DO

The West African Kingdoms have plenty to offer the traveler. Visit the bustling caravan cities for great shopping. You will also see amazing mud mosques. Enjoy a feast of music and dance at one of the region's many colorful festivals. Learn how to talk with the drums or strike it rich in the goldfields! There are few places in the world with so many things to see and do.

THE CARAVAN CITIES

You can take your pick of many interesting cities in the West African Kingdoms. The largest and most important ones are in the **savanna** regions. They are close to the Sahara Desert (see map, pages 4–5).

GAO

Gao, on the Niger River was once a fishing village. The best time to visit is about 500 years ago, between 1464 and 1591. Gao is then the capital of the mighty Songhai Empire. This big city has a good caravan trade. Don't miss the busy harbor or markets.

Today's lively market in the town of Mopti, Mali, is similar to those in the time of the West African Kingdoms.

TIMBUKTU

The important city of Timbuktu has grown rich from trade. Surprisingly, much of this rich city is a maze of dusty streets, though. But you will find an amazing palace and some great mud-built mosques. Arrive there well before sunset as the gates of the city are shut at night.

KOUMBI SALEH

Koumbi Saleh is the capital of the kingdom of Ghana. It is more like two cities in one. One city is the royal city. It is for the king and his followers. The king's richly decorated palace is at the very center of the royal city. There is also a second city about 6 miles (10 kilometers) away on the other side of the river. This city is for merchants and traders.

TEGHAZA

This very hot oasis is in the Sahara Desert. It is found about 400 miles (640 kilometers) north of Timbuktu. Teghaza must be one of the toughest places on Earth to live. Wars are fought to control it though. But why is it so important? Because ancient dried-up lakes nearby are the region's main source of salt. Go and look at the hundreds of slaves digging salt blocks out of the lake beds.

CITIES OF THE SAVANNA AND RAIN FOREST

The caravan cities aren't the only places worth visiting in the West African Kingdoms. There are also great cities on the **savanna** and in the **rain forest**.

DJENNÉ

Djenné is famous for its mud mosque (see pages 6–7). It is also probably the most attractive city you can visit on the savanna. The surrounding countryside is fertile, or good for growing crops. The city is on an island on the Bani River. It is a busy port with great markets. You'll see dozens of boats carrying goods on the 250-mile (400-

This beautiful terra-cotta figure of a man comes from the Djenné area.

kilometer) trip down the Bani and Niger rivers to Timbuktu. Here goods are transferred to **camel caravans**. Visit Djenné between the years 1200 and 1600. That is between 400 and 800 years ago.

A 17th-century Dutch traveler visited and drew Benin's royal palace.

BENIN CITY

Benin City is the most impressive rain forest city. The city has a massive wall more than 56 feet (17 meters) high all around it. Benin has a very long, wide main street with neat houses. Each of the city's nine gates has a tax collector. He takes tolls (payments) from visiting merchants.

Go and visit the royal palace. It has masses of rooms and courtyards. Benin is a very welcoming place to visitors. The best time to visit is between 1400 and 1800. That is between 200 and 600 years ago.

VISIT A GOLD MINE

The main source of wealth in the West African Kingdoms is gold. It is mined (dug out) of valleys in the Upper Niger, the Senega, and the Sirba rivers.

GOLD MINING

Gold is found using two methods. Miners dig pits directly into gold-bearing rock. Some pits can be more than 130 feet (40 meters) deep. The rocks are brought to the surface and crushed. The gold can then be removed by hand.

Another method is to find gold mixed in the mud and sand in riverbeds. People dig up the mud and sand with simple hand tools such as hoes and picks. Panning the gold (see box, opposite page) separates gold from mud and sand.

These weights and spoons are for weighing gold dust. They come from the Akan kingdoms of the **rain forest**.

THE KING'S SHARE

Even if you find a big, shiny gold nugget you won't be able to keep it. Guards are on the alert at gold mines. They will kill anyone trying to steal gold. All gold nuggets belong to the king. Miners can sell the gold dust they find, though. All this means the king is very wealthy. Because of these rules, the price of gold at the market also stays high.

This lovely gold brooch comes from the country of Senegal. It may be as much as 700 years old.

FESTIVALS

Festivals are important occasions. They celebrate harvests, religious beliefs, the passing of seasons, and young people entering adulthood. You will be able to join in on many of the festivals.

DEAD SOULS

You may be lucky enough to catch the Dogon people's Dama mask festival. This takes place every 12 years. Before the festival, men disappear to the caves. Here they mourn for dead souls. They make masks in the caves. The dead souls are believed to live in the masks. The masks ward off evil spirits. For five days the masked men give exciting dance performances.

These masked dancers are from the Dogon country.

MUSLIM FESTIVALS

The main festivals in **Muslim** areas are Eid al-Fitr and Eid al-Adha. Both are celebrated with prayers and spectacular royal parades. Eid al-Fitr celebrates the ending of Ramadan. It means the "the festival of breaking the **fast**." This is when people begin to eat again. It is also a time for exchanging gifts, giving to the poor, and visiting friends and relatives.

Eid al-Adha means "the festival of the sacrifice." It celebrates the **prophet** Abraham. He was prepared to sacrifice his son for God. All families sacrifice a sheep if they can afford it. They then give a share of the meat to the poor.

THE YAM FESTIVAL

The biggest festival for many **rain forest** people takes place at the beginning of August. It is a celebration of the **yam** harvest. The oldest man in the village has a special right. He eats the first yam of the harvest. The festival actually lasts for three days. There is always plenty of music and dancing. The people give thanks to the gods for the harvest that year.

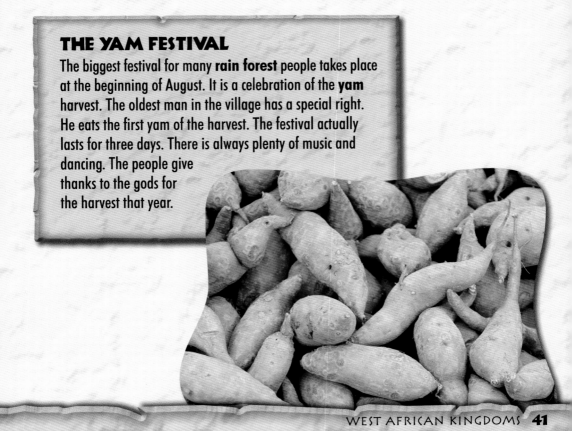

MUSIC, DANCE, AND STORYTELLING

The West African Kingdoms are great for music, dance, and exciting stories. You will hear music almost everywhere. People love to sing while hard at work. The rhythm (beat) helps them work together well—and time passes faster.

MUSICAL INSTRUMENTS

The music here is wonderful wherever you go. Musicians use many different instruments. They play flutes, elephant tusk horns, and **thumb pianos**. Thumb pianos have metal bars that can be played with the thumbs. They also enjoy playing bells, rattles, drums, and trumpets.

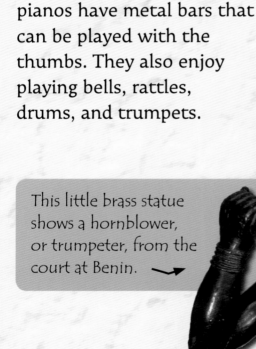

This little brass statue shows a hornblower, or trumpeter, from the court at Benin. ➜

HOW TO TALK WITH DRUMS

With talking drums people can send messages from one village to another—almost as quickly as a telephone call. Message drums are made out of hollow logs. They have a range of about 5 miles (8 kilometers). The drums can imitate the natural rhythms of human speech. Smaller talking drums are used in storytelling. A skilled drummer can make a sound similar to spoken words.

This is a Nigerian talking drum.

DANCE

You are sure to see some very exciting dances in the West African Kingdoms. There are dances for all sorts of religious festivals, weddings, and funerals. Male dancers wear wonderful masks to show different characters. Female dancers may only paint their faces. All dancers wear colorful costumes of woven grass, feathers, beads, and cloth.

SHOPPING

The **savanna**, the desert, and the **rain forest** each have different climates and resources. This means people have to trade with each other to get all they need. Salt comes from the desert. Grain and animal products come from the savanna. Wood, **ivory**, and gold come from the forests. Cloth, pottery, and glass may come from as far away as Europe and China. The markets are great opportunities to pick up souvenirs.

WHAT TO BUY

The West African Kingdoms are famous for their unique wood carvings and special ceremonial masks. Musical instruments, such as talking drums, also make great souvenirs. Don't buy any of the beautiful ivory bracelets and ornaments. These are carved from elephant tusks. This cruel trade (business) kills many elephants.

BRONZE SCULPTURE

Craftsworkers from the rain forest kingdoms of southern Nigeria are experts at making copper and bronze sculptures. Metalwork from the kingdom of Benin is excellent.

This **plaque** shows a hunter armed with a crossbow. It is a good example of Nigerian bronze work.

GOLD

Gold is the best buy in the West African Kingdoms. It is cheaper here than anywhere else. Bring something from home with you. You can then exchange it for gold when you arrive. Good-quality glass beads are highly valued for jewelry. You may want to bring a sack of these with you. You can even make a profit while on vacation in the West African Kingdoms!

MONEY

You cannot use coins in the West African Kingdoms. Cowrie shells (see box, below), cloth, blocks of salt, and gold and copper ingots (bars) are all used instead. You can manage without them, though. First agree on the value of an item in cowrie shells. Then pay the trader in goods of equal value.

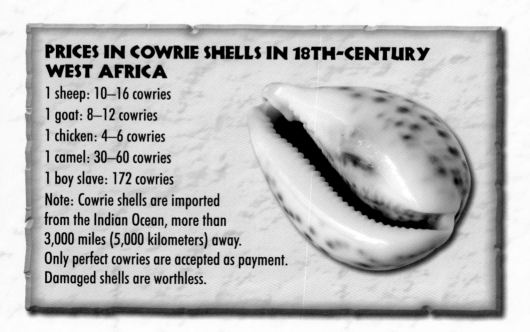

PRICES IN COWRIE SHELLS IN 18TH-CENTURY WEST AFRICA

1 sheep: 10–16 cowries
1 goat: 8–12 cowries
1 chicken: 4–6 cowries
1 camel: 30–60 cowries
1 boy slave: 172 cowries

Note: Cowrie shells are imported from the Indian Ocean, more than 3,000 miles (5,000 kilometers) away. Only perfect cowries are accepted as payment. Damaged shells are worthless.

Poisonous snakes like this green mamba are one of the hazards of travel in the West African Kingdoms. Some insects are even more dangerous!

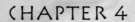

CHAPTER 4

LOOKING AFTER YOURSELF

You are unlikely to become a victim of crime in the West African Kingdoms. Also officials are usually honest and will treat you well. This region can be dangerous though, because of the many deadly tropical diseases. In wild areas you will also need to watch out for dangerous wildlife.

HEALTH AND DISEASE

Take some modern medicines and mosquito netting with you. They just may save your life during your visit to the West African Kingdoms. West Africans have greater **natural resistance** (ability to resist catching a disease) to tropical diseases. They are not **immune** (protected from disease or infection) to them. They just have a better chance of recovering.

LOCAL HEALERS

Most local people believe that diseases are caused by witchcraft or by angry **ancestor** spirits. These are souls of dead family members. Healers are experts at treating patients with herbal or plant medicines. They also use magic to send the angry spirit away.

A healer performs a dance. This is to drive away the evil spirits that cause sickness.

MALARIA

Malaria is a nasty disease. It will be the single greatest threat to your health in the West African Kingdoms. Malaria is caused by a **parasite**. A parasite is an animal (or sometimes a plant) that lives on another. It gets food from it.

Mosquitoes carry the deadly malaria parasite. At the time of the great West African Kingdoms, no one knows that mosquitoes carry malaria. They do know that mosquitoes are pests, though! Local West Africans hang bunches of strong-smelling leaves over their doors. This may help to keep the mosquitoes away. If you do get malaria, make sure you visit a local healer fast. Scientists have now proved that some traditional herbal medicines can help with this disease.

THE DEADLY TSETSE FLY

One of the deadliest pests in the West African Kingdoms is the tsetse fly. Like the mosquito, it carries a deadly parasite. The parasite can cause a fatal sleeping sickness in humans.

Tropical forests and riverbanks are the worst places for tsetse flies. There is one good thing though. Tsetse flies don't bite at night. The locals travel after sunset in these regions. Make sure you do the same.

Weather conditions can make travel dangerous in the West African Kingdoms. High winds can cause sandstorms like this one in Mali.

PERSONAL SAFETY

The cities of West African Kingdoms are quite safe for visitors. Watchmen patrol the streets at night. Others are stationed in the marketplace to guard stores and warehouses. Officials are usually honest and do not demand **bribes**. A bribe is when an official asks you for money—for nothing!

CRIME AND PUNISHMENT

Minor crimes are punished by fines or a painful beating on the soles of the feet. Murder, violent robbery, and cattle stealing are all punished with death.

If a criminal injures someone, he has to care for his victim. If the victim doesn't recover, the criminal is executed. If the victim recovers, the criminal will get a fine and a beating.

CANNIBALISM

Locals in the West African Kingdoms do not eat people for food. Even so, you are sure to hear a bloodcurdling tale or two about cannibals eating human flesh. These stories are just to frighten visitors. Human flesh is sometimes eaten as part of rituals in traditional African religions, however. The flesh comes from people who have died naturally.

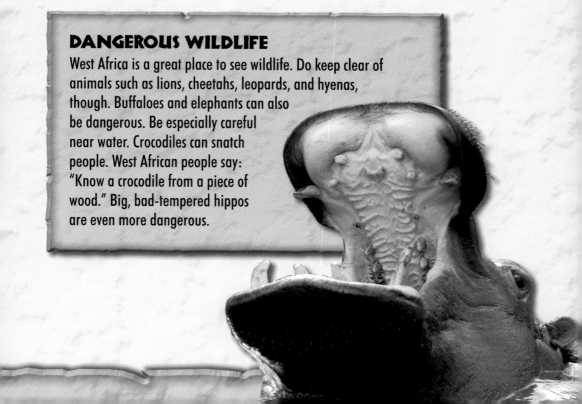

DANGEROUS WILDLIFE

West Africa is a great place to see wildlife. Do keep clear of animals such as lions, cheetahs, leopards, and hyenas, though. Buffaloes and elephants can also be dangerous. Be especially careful near water. Crocodiles can snatch people. West African people say: "Know a crocodile from a piece of wood." Big, bad-tempered hippos are even more dangerous.

The bright colors of this traditional patterned cloth have always been popular in the West African Kingdoms.

CHAPTER 5

USEFUL INFORMATION

Writing was not widely used in the West African Kingdoms. Much of our information about the kingdoms comes from visitors. Arab merchants and European explorers didn't always respect West Africans. You can easily show respect for the West African people you meet. One way is to learn some of their languages. This will also help you make friends during your travels.

WEST AFRICAN LANGUAGES

Try speaking the local language. You will enjoy your trip more this way. The West African Kingdoms have an amazing variety of **ethnic groups**. They speak dozens of different languages. One widely understood non-African language in **Muslim** areas is Arabic.

THE FULANI

The Fulani are one of the most widespread peoples of West Africa. They live mainly by herding. They feed and keep their animals together. Most Fulani are Muslims. Their language is called Fulfulde.

THE MALINKE

The Malinke are the ruling people of the great kingdom of Mali. The Malinke and many others speak the Mande language. It is a useful language to learn.

THE SONGHAI

The Songhai have settled along the middle Niger River. They live by herding, farming, fishing, and trade. The Songhai language is very different from others.

THE YORUBA

The Yoruba language comes from a group of languages. The Yoruba live in the Nigerian **rain forest**.

THE HAUSA

The Hausa live on the **savanna** of northern Nigeria. The Hausa live by cattle rearing and by trade. Hausa merchants have settled right across West Africa. Their language is a very useful one for travelers to the kingdoms to learn.

HAUSA WORDS AND PHRASES

English	Hausa	Counting:	
Greetings	*Salamu alaikum*	1	*daya*
Good afternoon	*Barka da yamma*	2	*biyu*
How much?	*Nawa nawa ne?*	3	*uku*
That's expensive	*Kai, suna da tsada*	4	*hudu*
Did you sleep well?	*Ina kwana?*	5	*biyar*
Fine	*Lafiya lau*	6	*shida*
water	*ruwa*	7	*bakwai*
food	*abinci*	8	*takwas*
meat	*nama*	9	*tara*
milk	*madara*	10	*goma*
market	*kasura*	11	*goma sha daya*
money	*kudi*	20	*ashirin*
man	*namiji*	21	*ashirin da daya*
woman	*mata*	30	*talatin*
child/children	*yaro*	40	*arba'in*
mother	*uwa*	50	*hamsin*
father	*uba*	60	*sittin*
house	*gida*	70	*saba'in*
clothes	*tufafi*	80	*tamanin*
camel caravan	*azalai*	90	*casa'in*
sand dune	*erg*	100	*dari*
		200	*dari biyu*

HOW DO WE KNOW ABOUT WEST AFRICAN HISTORY?

For much of their history, writing was not used in the West African Kingdoms. Because of this, we rely on what visitors have written about them. Writing in native languages and Arabic only became widespread about 400 years ago. Books by West African writers today tell much about past history and customs of the people. Many of these stories were originally passed down by word of mouth.

WRITTEN HISTORIES

Muslim families used to write down their histories. These were typically written in Arabic or the local Songhai language about 300 years ago. These written histories are often beautifully decorated with **geometric** patterns and gold letters. Geometric patterns are simple shapes like squares and circles. There are no pictures. This is because the Islamic religion does not encourage the art of pictures.

DIGGING UP THE PAST

Archaeological excavations (digs) are an important way of finding out about the West African Kingdoms. Simple objects show a lot about how people lived. We know what their houses were like. We know what they ate. And we know how they treated their dead.

ARAB WRITERS

Many Arab writers from North Africa and the Middle East visited the West African Kingdoms. A Moroccan, Ibn Battuta (1304–1369), visited West Africa in 1352. His detailed accounts are interesting. He does have unfair prejudices against Africans though. For example, he thought of Africans only as slaves.

WORD OF MOUTH

West Africa has a strong tradition of oral history. People pass on history by word of mouth from one generation to the next. They use their own well-trained memories. Stories are often turned into poems. This makes them easier to remember.

FORMER SLAVES

Some Europeans bought African slaves. The slaves were taught to read and write. A few later wrote accounts of their awful experiences as slaves. The best known is Olaudah Equiano (1745–1797). At age 11, he was kidnapped in Nigeria and sold as a slave. Equiano eventually bought his freedom. He went to live in England. His autobiography (own story) is called *The Interesting Narrative of the Life of Olaudah Equiano* (1789).

WHAT HAPPENED TO THE WEST AFRICAN KINGDOMS?

About 400 years ago, the West African Kingdoms began to **decline**. The Atlantic Ocean slave trade and European **colonialism** were big factors. Colonialism brought groups of settlers from other countries. There were also holy wars between **Muslim** kingdoms and their non-Muslim neighbors.

KIDNAPPED!

Don't travel alone in remote country. People, including travelers, are sometimes kidnapped and sold into slavery. Slavers may also sneak into villages during the day and try to snatch any children. This is when most adults are working in the fields. It is then easy for the kidnappers to tie up and carry a child away.

REASONS FOR DECLINE

The first West African Kingdoms to decline were those in the north. New sea trade routes by Europeans took trade away from routes across the Sahara Desert. Kingdoms with control over this trade became much poorer. Others were raided by stronger kingdoms.

Prisoners became slaves. In 200 years, more than 20 million West Africans were sold to European slave traders. The slave traders took only the healthiest and strongest young people. This huge loss of people held back growth in the region.

The holy wars were called **jihads**. Jihads over 100 years ago (in the 19th century) caused further problems. Medical improvements at this time also finally allowed Europeans to live in West Africa without falling ill. Because of this, and newly invented weapons such as machine guns, Europeans were able to conquer the West African Kingdoms.

This painting is of Freetown in Sierra Leone. It is a settlement for freed slaves. It was founded by the British government in the 1780s.

WEST AFRICAN HISTORY AT A GLANCE

TIMELINE

200 BCE–CE 400	The first towns and cities develop in the region.
100 BCE	Introduction of camels to the Sahara Desert. This increases trade between North and West Africa.
Around CE 500	Foundation of the kingdom of Ghana. This is the first large kingdom in West Africa.
Around 570–632	The life of Muhammad, the **prophet** of **Islam**.
Around 750	**Muslim** merchants from North Africa begin to visit to buy slaves, gold, and **ivory**.
Around 1000	The Islamic religion begins to gain **converts** in West Africa.
Around 1250	Kingdom of Benin is founded.
1312–1337	Mansa Musa rules Mali.
1352	The Moroccan Ibn Battuta writes about his travels in West Africa.
Around 1400	Timbuktu becomes an important center of Muslim learning.
1440–1473	Benin becomes a powerful empire.
1464–1492	Songhai becomes a great kingdom (under Sonni Ali).
1517	Beginning of the Atlantic Ocean slave trade. (Spain begins sending regular shipments of slaves to its American colonies.)
1591	Songhai is conquered by Morocco.
1807	Great Britain declares the slave trade to be illegal.
1884–1885	European powers agree to divide Africa between themselves.
1897	Great Britain conquers the kingdom of Benin.

FURTHER READING

BOOKS

Barr, Gary E. *West African Kingdoms* (Hands-on Ancient History). Chicago: Heinemann Library, 2006

Haskins, James and Kathleen Benson. *African Beginnings*. New York City: Amistad Press, 2007

Reece, Katherine E. *West African Kingdoms: Empires of Gold and Trade* (Ancient Civilizations). Vero Beach: Rourke, 2005

Shuter, Jane. *Ancient West African Kingdoms* (History Opens Windows). Chicago: Heinemann Library, 2008

WEBSITES

- exploringafrica.matrix.msu.edu/students/ curriculum/m7a/activity3.php
  This website includes a map showing the location of the West African Kingdoms, as well as many other kingdoms and empires throughout African history.

- www.bbc.co.uk/worldservice/africa/features/ storyofafrica/
  This website tells the story of the whole African continent, including the West African Kingdoms.

GLOSSARY

ancestor relative from long ago, or person someone is descended from

bribe gift or money offered to persuade someone to do something—usually something dishonest

caftan long, loose garment usually made of cotton

camel caravan line of camels that travel across the desert

cavalry soldiers who fight on horseback

civilization advanced state of society or culture, usually in the past

colonialism when a country establishes groups of settlers in other countries

convert someone who begins to follow a particular religion

decline fade, get worse, or slide downward

ethnic group cultural or national group; a people

fast stop eating food for a certain amount of time, often as a religious duty

geometric to do with simple shapes, such as squares and circles

humidity moisture or dampness in the air

immune protected from disease or infection

Islam religion founded by the prophet Muhammad. Muslim followers have one god, called Allah.

ivory hard, white material that makes up the tusks of elephants, hippos, and walruses

jihad Muslim holy war, fought to defend or spread the Islamic religion

litter bed or seat with handles, used to carry rich or important people, or those who are sick or injured

millet grain with small, hard kernals

minaret tower on a mosque, used by preachers to call Muslims to prayer

Muslim follower of Islam

natural resistance person's ability to resist catching a disease

oasis area in a desert with water and trees

parasite animal or plant that lives on or in another animal or plant (the host) and gets its nourishment from it. This often harms the host, weakening it or causing illness.

plantain green-skinned bananalike fruit

plaque ornamental plate that is fastened to a wall

prophet someone who is divinely inspired, or speaks for his god

rain forest dense tropical forest found in areas with high rainfall

savanna tropical grassland with scattered bushes and trees, and small patches of woodland

scurvy disease caused by a lack of vitamin C

thumb piano musical instrument with thin metal bars that are plucked with the thumb to play a tune

yam starchy root vegetable, similar to a sweet potato

INDEX